Chakra Mantra Magick

Tap Into The Magick Of Your Chakras

Copyright information

Copyright © 2015 by Baal Kadmon

All rights reserved. No part of this book may be reproduced by any mechanical, photographic, or electrical process, or in the form of a recording. Nor may it be stored in a storage/retrieval system nor transmitted or otherwise be copied for private or public use-other than "fair use" as quotations in articles or reviews—without the prior written consent of the Author.

The Information in this book is solely for educational purposes and not for the treatment, diagnosis or prescription of any diseases. This text is not meant to provide financial or health advice of any sort. The Author and the publisher are in no way liable for any use or misuse of the material. No Guarantee of results are being made in this text.

Kadmon, Baal

Chakra Mantra Magick - Tap Into The Magick Of Your Chakras
—1st ed

Printed in the United States of America

Cover image : #82299922 © brizz666 - Fotolia.com

Book Cover Design: Baal Kadmon

At the best of our ability we have credited those who created the pictures based on the research we have conducted. If there are images in the book that have not been given due copyright notice please contact us at Resheph@baalkadmon.com and we will remedy the situation by giving proper copyright credit or we will remove the image/s at your request.

INTRODUCTION

It is said that when one balances their chakras, the rest of their life falls into place. This is very true, but there is much more than chakra balancing to strive for. Chakras themselves can be a source of energy to create magick. Using Chakras for Magick makes perfect sense. Since spiritual and physical energies travel via the chakras. You are, in essence , your chakras. Everything in the world , whether this world or the spiritual world communicates with you via your chakras. Everything you have in this life or don't have for that matter are a result of your chakras. In this book, we will perform 7 rituals, 1 for every chakra. We are not so much looking to balance or clear our chakras, what we will be doing is using the chakras as magickal vehicles to attain what we desire. Let us proceed.

WHAT ARE CHAKRAS?

The very word Chakra comes from the Sanskrit word *cakram,* which means wheel. In Hindu art the chakras are often depicted as flowers, each with a set number of petals. These flower petals are interconnected in such a way that they appear as spokes in an energetic wheel, they are visualized as whirling wheels of energy situated along the spine in what is called the "Subtle Body". The subtle body is your energetic double as it were. This double is not fully outside of you, but is intertwined with your physical body. Due to this intertwining with the body, the energy flowing through the subtle body affects everything in the physical body as well. These Chakra energy centers are moving and swirling clockwise and are the main avenue for the reception and transmission of energy both physically and spiritually as I stated in the introduction.

We have ancient Hindu texts to thank for the discovery of the chakras. Some of these texts may be the oldest text in existence. There are 7 chakra centers in our bodies, some traditions say that we have more, but for our purposes we will deal with the more common view that we have 7 chakras. Perhaps in a future book we will discuss other chakras systems.

Each Chakra has a color and a mantra, mainly a seed syllable or a single letter ascribed to them. We will be using the mantra as the sound of magick in each ritual, we will also be using the color as well. In addition, at the end of each chakra description I will also indicate how we will use the mantra.

I will now describe each chakra as well as supply an image that has their respective seed mantras present. We will be using these images in the rituals as well.

The Root Chakra

Our first chakra is known as the root Chakra. In Sanskrit this chakra is known as Muladhara. The root chakra is our foundational chakra and can be found at the very end of our spine and right atop the genitals.

The color associated with this chakra is red. Red can be a vital and living color but can also be associated with anger and frustration. Since this a foundational chakra the element that it most closely resonates is with earth. This chakra, when balanced, will keep us grounded.

Since this chakra is at our lower extremities, it will influence those regions.

This chakra has a profound influence on the digestive system, especially the lower digestive system as well as the kidneys and adrenal glands. If you have issues with any of these areas, it may be partially due to a block in this chakra. A block often manifests in sluggishness, fatigue, constipation. It is responsible for insomnia, lower back pain , eating issues on both spectrums. Emotionally, an imbalance will often lead to depression, instability, irritability and anger, addiction and irrational fearfulness.

If all is well in this chakra, you feel secure, grounded, your body functions properly and waste is efficiently released from your body. Often a balanced Root is also associated with financial wellbeing . Without money in this world, you cannot be secure. A balanced root chakra will be very helpful here.

Seed Sound for this Chakra: Lam.
Color: Red.
Ritual Purpose: To Attract Money

The Sacral Chakra

The Sacral chakra is our second one. In Sanskrit is called Swadhisthana. This chakra is located in and around the lower abdomen; approximately 2 inches below the navel. The color associated with this chakra is Orange.

This chakra is highly connected to our emotional life. It has a profound influence on them. And like emotions, this chakras element is water. The body location of this chakra most closely influences the ovaries and testicular regions of the body. Similar to the root chakra, this one can also influence the kidneys and stomach, in addition to the pancreas, spleen, gallbladder and liver.

This chakra influences our sexuality, our general emotional states, our interpersonal relationships and our own acceptance of ourselves.

If this chakra is out of balance, several physical and emotional issues may arise. Such as , low libido , impotence, lower back pain, hormonal imbalances, urinary tract infections, fatigue and generalized pain in the lower extremities. Emotionally, one may experience excessive need for control and perfectionism. Increased irritability, excessive shyness, enhanced states of guilt and shame that can lead to addiction. If you ever feel stifled creativity, this too can be an imbalance in this chakra.

If this chakra is balanced, it can be quite beautiful. You can experience increased sexuality and the ability to expertise true intimacy and take pleasure in the things that you do. Your relationships will be harmonious and without drama. A balanced Second chakra essentially imparts a joy for life.

Seed Sound: VAM

Color: Orange.

Ritual: To Increase and attract sexual energy

The Solar Plexus Chakra

The third chakra is the solar plexus chakra. Its located between the bottom of your rib cage and your navel. I tend to visualize right at or above the navel area. This chakras name is Manipura and its color is yellow. This chakra represents our thinking mind and our ability to take action in life.

The physical area this charka governs are similar to the previous chakras; kidneys ,the gallbladder, liver, pancreas, spleen and also the mid-spine region and part of the little intestine. The major gland however is the pancreas.

If this chakra is out of balance , you may experience the following emotional issues. Low and very low self worth and esteem. Body image issues, but also your general image of yourself. This chakra, is imbalanced may also stifle your desire to take action and cause you to be timid about things.

If this chakra is not balanced you may experience physical issues such as bulimia or anorexia, liver issues, colon issues. Ulcers, pancreas issues as well as arthritis.

If the chakra is balanced, the opposite of the above would be true. Your mind will be clear, you will have healthy self worth , strong positive desire for life and a strong sense of self. Not to mention, your organs will work more efficiently, especially your pancreas which will help your blood sugar. When blood sugar is stabilized your mental and physical states are also stabilized and you won't feel or experience wild swings in mood, energy or appetite for that matter.

Seed Sound: RAM
Color: Yellow
Ritual: To Increase Self Esteem

The Heart Chakra

The fourth chakra or Heart Chakra called Anāhata in Sanskrit Is situated in the center of the chest just right of the heart area itself.

The heart, throughout all human history has always been associated as the seat of love and sometimes seat of the soul. It is a major chakra and is often at the center of the chakras since it distills the lower chakras energies so it may move up and relaxes the energy from the higher chakras when traveling down to the lower chakras.

The color that is most associated with this chakra is green but some traditions also ascribe the color pink to this chakra.

Aside from the heart itself, this chakra also governs the arms, hands, shoulders, the lungs, breasts and the entire circulatory system.

When this chakra is out of balance it can wreak havoc on the emotions. Deep feeling of despair may be experienced where hope doesn't exist. If you find it too difficult to open up and love can also be a symptom of an imbalance in this chakra. Like the root chakra, this imbalance can lead to anger, hatred and fear.

When this chakra is out of balance it can lead to heart problems, various pulmonary diseases of which asthma is a part of. Pain the shoulders, arms. May even cause breast cancer, but also growths of a noncancerous type as well.

A balanced heart chakra, often appears as a sense of nurturing, optimism, compassion and feelings of wholeness with oneself. But also connectedness to others and the ability to love another. Often this chakra is hurt more often than others because of life events. Heartbreak, grief etc can really throw this chakra out of balance.

Seed Sound: YAM
Color: Green
Ritual: To Attract A Mate

The Throat Chakra

The fifth chakra or Throat Chakra called Viśuddha in Sanskrit Is situated in the throat area itself. This chakras color is blue. This chakra is the chakra of communication and expression. Since it is located at the throat, the corresponding organ to this chakra is the thyroid. This tiny organ regulate our metabolism and if it is imbalanced can cause either unhealthy weight loss or weight gain. It also has a role in memory, energy levels or lack thereof. This chakra is also center around the vocal cords, the neck and nearby areas.

If the throat chakra is not balanced, this can seriously influence your creativity, your ability to express yourself verbally. Often people with imbalanced throat chakra find it hard to speak up and this builds up and often these people develop thyroid problems. On the other extreme, it can also display itself as a lack of control when it comes to speech. So the person with an imbalanced chakra may speak too much. it can work both ways. Other manifestations of this imbalance involve dishonesty and being overly harsh and critical and on the flip side, under spoken or too soft spoken for our own good. As I stated earlier, the thyroid tends to be the one hit hardest by an imbalanced throat chakra. The second most common illness associated with an imbalanced chakra are throat issues in general. I know of a person who stifles her emotions and has had a hard time speaking up for herself. It manifested by frequent bouts of strep throat, tonsillitis, ear infections and related issues. Although she does not know about the chakras, one thing is for certain, when she took back her power, interestingly enough, her throat issues went away. She did connect her throat issues with her communication issues but not in terms of it being a chakra issue. In either case, the results are quite dramatic. She even started to get in shape because she no longer had negative communication with her own psyche.

When this chakra is balanced, communication flows easily, your creativity is sparked and the ease to which it flows is very noticeable. When this chakra is balanced, you are able to create boundaries with people and have the ability to speak your mind. Self awareness also becomes easier since your inner communication channels are not blocked.

Seed Sound: HAM
Color: Blue
Ritual: To Strengthen Your ability to Ask for what You want and Find Your voice

The Third Eye Chakra or Brow Chakra

The sixth chakra or Brow Chakra called Ājñā in Sanskrit Is situated right between the eyes. This is by far the most popular of the chakras, most people have heard of the third eye and for good reason. This is the eye of discernment and wisdom, your mind's eye if you will. This chakra is represented by the beautiful color of indigo.

The gland that this chakra most connects to is the pituitary gland. This gland regulates many aspects of the body including how tall you will be, your skin coloring and various aspects of childbirth. It is often called the master gland because it has a profound effect on all the other glands and hormones in your body. Since the 3rd eye is positioned right between the eyes, the brain , eyes and nose are also within its jurisdiction so to speak.

If this chakra is not balanced it can be devastating. Often an imbalanced third eye has been associated with ADHD, certain mental illnesses that cause disassociation with reality. Judgment in general can be impaired leading to confusion and "brain fog".

Physically, the imbalance can show in alarming ways. Often severally imbalanced 3rd eye can lead to panic attacks, brain tumors, migraine headaches, various learning disabilities, strokes and other ischemic attacks, as well as severe nightmares and the like.

if this chakra is balanced, we gain tremendous physical and mental benefits. Our intuition will be heightened, our ability to manifest our thoughts for good is also more apparent. Our concentration will be laser-like. It can open a completely new world for you. Both the inner and outer world.

Seed Sound: OM

Color: Indigo

Ritual: To enhance Your Intuition and psychic abilities.

The Crown Chakra

The seventh chakra or Crown Chakra called Sahasrāra in Sanskrit Is situated right at the top of the head. This chakra serves as your spiritual gateway. It is also the location where life/divine energy enters into the chakra system and your body. It is no coincidence that in almost every religion, gods, prophets and holy people all had light shine from the tops of their heads in the form of halos. That shine is from a developed Crown Chakra. An imbalance in the Crown Chakra can cause self centeredness, but a special form of self centeredness called Spiritual narcissism. Spiritual narcissism develops when a person has such a strong sense of spirituality that instead of channeling that for the benefit of others it translates into feelings of superiority. This is very pervasive in the self help community. An imbalance at this chakra can also lead to some astounding delusions. When this chakra is developed we experience deep understanding, spiritual connection and bliss. This level has no concern for duality. It has transcended both time and space. When balanced, we become more selfless, more connected to the divine and more loving towards all of existence. This chakra , like the third eye also over sees the brain and many of the same symptoms of imbalance are presented.

Seed Sound: OM

Color: Violet

Ritual: To gain direct CONTROL and Communication with Spiritual beings.

Now that You know what each chakra is and what we will use them for, let us discuss what you will need for the rituals.

WHAT YOU WILL NEED

Before we proceed, here is a list of thing you can use to enhance your Chakra Magick **(IF YOU DO NOT HAVE THESE ITEMS IT IS PERFECTLY OKAY, THEY SIMPLY ENHANCE YOUR RITUAL)**

1. An image of the Chakra. I have enclosed the images in this book. You will see them as we go through the material.

2. Any Incense you desire

3. The following Candles: Red Votive Candles Orange Votive Candles Yellow Votive Candles Green Votive Candles Blue Votive Candles Chakra Votive Indigo Candle Violet Votive Candles **(I just happen to like these but you can get any brand of candles you like)**

4. A secure plate or candle holder to hold the candles. Since the ones I recommend vary in size you can use the a make or brand of your choosing. Just make sure to find one that will hold these candles and will allow for safety (NEVER LEAVE CANDLES BURNING UNATTENDED)

5. An Incense holder. (NEVER LEAVE INCENSE BURNING UNATTENDED)

TIBETAN BUDDHIST MEDITATION 108 BEADS: I will explain below.

Let me now explain the rationale behind the objects above.

1. An image of the Chakra, this will help focus the mind.

2. Incense, this just creates a pleasant atmosphere. Incense has a way to make the surroundings holy.

3. **Candles: (Please note you can buy any kind of candle you like, they don't have to be chimes or votive. I just happen to like the ones I am providing below)**

Each color represents a chakra. In order they are Root, Sacral, Solar Plexus, Heart, Throat , Third Eye and Crown

Root:

Red Votive Candles

Sacral:

Orange Votive Candles

Solar Plexus:

Yellow Votive Candles

Heart:

Green Votive Candles

Throat:

Blue Votive Candles

Third Eye:

Chakra Votive Indigo Candle

Crown :

Violet Votive Candles

TIBETAN BUDDHIST MEDITATION 108 BEADS: This is optional, but if you are looking to really gain mastery over your chakras, it is a good idea to get beads so you can recite the chakra mantras often. I will explain this in the chapter on "Siddhi" later this book.

CHAKRA MAGICK RITUALS

Below you will find 7 rituals, very simple but powerful ones. Each ritual can be done at anytime.

I will walk you through each ritual step by step... In order for these to work, please perform these once a day until you have achieved your goal. The ritual/s may work right away, if so, then you will not need to do them again unless you desire to.

ROOT CHAKRA MAGICK

Please setup a place in your abode that you can dedicate to this ritual. If you have an altar, that is superb but if you don't, any place in your home where the ritual can be performed is good too.

Image of Chakra:

1. Look at the image of the Chakra

2. Place the Red candle in the middle of your altar and light it.

3. In the back, please light the incense.

4. Sit quietly and think about your desire to attain financial assistance

5. Say the following Mantra WITH PASSION SEVERAL TIMES UNTIL YOU FEEL IT OVERTAKE YOU: **LAM**

6. Now focus on the chakra image as you recite the mantra

7. When you are satisfied, you may let the candle/s and incense burn to completion. (Please be sure not to leave them unattended. If you need to leave your abode, you may extinguishing them and ignite them upon your return.)

Thus concludes this ritual. You have woken up your root chakra.

SACRAL CHAKRA MAGICK

Please setup a place in your abode that you can dedicate to this ritual. If you have an altar, that is superb but if you don't, any place in your home where the ritual can be performed is good too.

Image of Chakra:

1. Look at the image of the Chakra

2. Place the Orange candle in the middle of your altar and light it.

3. In the back, please light the incense.

4. Sit quietly and think about your desire to increase your sexual energy and attraction

5. Say the following Mantra WITH PASSION SEVERAL TIMES UNTIL YOU FEEL IT OVERTAKE YOU: **VAM**

6. Now focus on the chakra image as you recite the mantra

7. When you are satisfied, you may let the candle/s and incense burn to completion. (Please be sure not to leave them unattended. If you need to leave your abode, you may extinguishing them and ignite them upon your return.)

Thus concludes this ritual. You have woken up your sacral chakra, you may feel a surge in sexual energy. Do something about it :)

SOLAR PLEXUS CHAKRA MAGICK

Please setup a place in your abode that you can dedicate to this ritual. If you have an altar, that is superb but if you don't, any place in your home where the ritual can be performed is good too.

Image of Chakra:

1. Look at the image of the Chakra

2. Place the yellow candle in the middle of your altar and light it.

3. In the back, please light the incense.

4. Sit quietly and think about your desire to increase your confidence and self worth

5. Say the following Mantra WITH PASSION SEVERAL TIMES UNTIL YOU FEEL IT OVERTAKE YOU: **RAM**

6. Now focus on the chakra image as you recite the mantra

7. When you are satisfied, you may let the candle/s and incense burn to completion. (Please be sure not to leave them unattended. If you need to leave your abode, you may extinguishing them and ignite them upon your return.)

Thus concludes this ritual. You have woken up solar plexus, do you feel more confident?

HEART CHAKRA MAGICK

Please setup a place in your abode that you can dedicate to this ritual. If you have an altar, that is superb but if you don't, any place in your home where the ritual can be performed is good too.

Image of Chakra:

1. Look at the image of the Chakra

2. Place the green candle in the middle of your altar and light it.

3. In the back, please light the incense.

4. Sit quietly and think about your desire to attract a mate into your life

5. Say the following Mantra WITH PASSION SEVERAL TIMES UNTIL YOU FEEL IT OVERTAKE YOU: **YAM**

6. Now focus on the chakra image as you recite the mantra

7. When you are satisfied, you may let the candle/s and incense burn to completion. (Please be sure not to leave them unattended. If you need to leave your abode, you may extinguishing them and ignite them upon your return.)

Thus concludes this ritual. You are now resonating with the energy of love, this will help you attract the mate of your dreams

THROAT CHAKRA MAGICK

Please setup a place in your abode that you can dedicate to this ritual. If you have an altar, that is superb but if you don't, any place in your home where the ritual can be performed is good too.

Image of Chakra:

1. Look at the image of the Chakra

2. Place the blue candle in the middle of your altar and light it.

3. In the back, please light the incense.

4. Sit quietly and think about your need to enhance your communication abilities and to gain courage to speak your word

5. Say the following Mantra WITH PASSION SEVERAL TIMES UNTIL YOU FEEL IT OVERTAKE YOU: **HAM**

6. Now focus on the chakra image as you recite the mantra

7. When you are satisfied, you may let the candle/s and incense burn to completion. (Please be sure not to leave them unattended. If you need to leave your abode, you may extinguishing them and ignite them upon your return.)

Thus concludes this ritual. You are now resonating with the energy of communication and courage. You will find your voice.

THIRD EYE CHAKRA MAGICK

Please setup a place in your abode that you can dedicate to this ritual. If you have an altar, that is superb but if you don't, any place in your home where the ritual can be performed is good too.

Image of Chakra:

1. Look at the image of the Chakra

2. Place the indigo candle in the middle of your altar and light it.

3. In the back, please light the incense.

4. Sit quietly and think about your desire to enhance your intuition and psychic abilities

5. Say the following Mantra WITH PASSION SEVERAL TIMES UNTIL YOU FEEL IT OVERTAKE YOU: **OM**

6. Now focus on the chakra image as you recite the mantra

7. When you are satisfied, you may let the candle/s and incense burn to completion. (Please be sure not to leave them unattended. If you need to leave your abode, you may extinguishing them and ignite them upon your return.)

Thus concludes this ritual. You will notice a marked increase in your psychic and intuitive powers.

CROWN CHAKRA MAGICK

Please setup a place in your abode that you can dedicate to this ritual. If you have an altar, that is superb but if you don't, any place in your home where the ritual can be performed is good too.

Image of Chakra:

1. Look at the image of the Chakra

2. Place the indigo candle in the middle of your altar and light it.

3. In the back, please light the incense.

4. Sit quietly and think about your desire TO CONTROL SPIRITUAL ENTITIES

5. Say the following Mantra WITH PASSION SEVERAL TIMES UNTIL YOU FEEL IT OVERTAKE YOU: **OM**

6. Now focus on the chakra image as you recite the mantra

7. When you are satisfied, you may let the candle/s and incense burn to completion. (Please be sure not to leave them unattended. If you need to leave your abode, you may extinguishing them and ignite them upon your return.)

Thus concludes this ritual. You will notice a marked increase in your power to summon and control spiritual forces.

HOW TO ENHANCE YOUR CHAKRA MAGICK PRACTICE - ACHIEVING SIDDHI

(Excerpted from Vashikaran Magick with some adjustments) Now that you have learned the chakra mantras, I want to add some additional information here that will really up the effectiveness of these mantras and any mantra practice for that matter. As you saw, most of the mantras can be recited a few times and some, many more times. When doing so, you compound the energy upon itself and then it produces results. Its like a charge builds up and eventually fires, producing the goal. This is generally how mantras work and often once the result is achieved, the energy dissipates and that will be the end of the ritual. But what if you could ALWAYS embody the energy of the mantra? There is a way and It is called Siddhi.

Siddhi, in Sanskrit means " perfection" "accomplishment" and "Attainment" of magical abilities. When one achieves Siddhi with a particular mantra they acquire the actual energy of that mantra. So for example, the Main Attraction Seed Mantra is "Kleem". If you recite this 10,000 times in one sitting, you will have mastered the energy of this mantra and your attraction abilities will be enhanced and things will come naturally to you. After you achieve Siddhi, you will be unstoppable, with every recitation of the mantra after Siddhi you are a true and effective magician. Some schools of thought say that you do not need to do all 10,000 in one sitting but over 40 days. Follow your intuition on whether you want to do these chants in one sitting or several.

In saying this, if you want to enhance any of these mantras, I suggest chanting them 1,000 to 10,000 times in one sitting. I know this sounds like a lot, but once you get into the groove with the mantra the recitation will move very quickly. To keep track of this, I suggest you use Mala beads. I personally use this brand:

TIBETAN BUDDHIST MEDITATION 108 BEADS

It has 108 beads; 108 is a sacred number and common in Hindu chanting. Although some of the mantras in this book require fewer than 108 recitation; I highly suggest you chant a mantra at least 108 times a day. With these Mala Beads, it will be easy to keep track. If you do 10 rounds of 108 recitations, you will be on your way to achieving Siddhi. You can, of course use any mala beads or create your own.

Conclusion

What you have learned here are the root sounds and rituals that will help you use your chakras to enhance your life and manifest things into it magickally. You can do anything with this power, not just what we covered in this book. These mantras are like electricity, the energy will flow in the direction of the intended output. In saying that please be firm in your intentions and make absolutely sure what you want is truly what you want. Your Chakras, once they get going, will work very quickly. Be very clear in your mind.

As they say, be careful what you ask for, you just might get it.

Other Books By The Author

The Mantra Magick Series:

VASHIKARAN MAGICK - LEARN THE DARK MANTRAS OF SUBJUGATION

Kali Mantra Magick: Summoning The Dark Powers of Kali Ma

Seed Mantra Magick: Master The Primordial Sounds of The universe

The Scared Names Series:

THE 72 NAMES OF GOD - THE 72 KEYS OF TRANSFORMATION

THE 72 ANGELS OF THE NAME - CALLING ON THE 72 ANGELS OF GOD

THE 99 NAMES OF ALLAH - ACQUIRING THE 99 DIVINE QUALITIES OF GOD

THE HIDDEN NAMES OF GENESIS - TAP INTO THE HIDDEN POWER OF MANIFESTATION

Magick Of the Saints Series

Mary Magick: Calling Forth The Divine Mother For Help

The Magick of Saint Expedite: Tap Into the Truly Miraculous Power of Saint Expedite

DISCLAIMER

Disclaimer: By law, I need to add this statement. This volume of "Mantra Magick" is for educational purposes only and does not claim to prevent or cure any disease. The advice and methods in this book should not be construed as financial, medical or psychological treatment. Please seek advice from a professional if you have serious financial, medical or psychological issues.

By purchasing, reading and or listening to this book, you understand that results are not guaranteed. In light of this, you understand that in the event that this book or audio does not work or causes harm in any area of your life, you agree that you do not hold Baal Kadmon, Amazon, its employees or affiliates liable for any damages you may experience or incur.

The Text and or Audio in this series are copyrighted 2015